www.finishinglinepress.com

Opia

poems by

Marjorie Sanders

Finishing Line Press
Georgetown, Kentucky

Opia

ACKNOWLEDGMENTS

Sanders, Marjorie. "Smile More." *Rebloom*, edited by Nikki Marrone, Point
Positive Publishing, 2020, p. 25.

Publisher: Leah Huete de Maines
Editor: Christen Kincaid
Cover Art: Vandy Pacetti-Donelson
Author Photo: Kayla Steade
Cover Design: Elizabeth Maines McCleavy

Order online: www.finishinglinepress.com
also available on amazon.com

Author inquiries and mail orders:
Finishing Line Press
PO Box 1626
Georgetown, Kentucky 40324
USA

Table of Contents

Blow.. 2

Dessert 3

PS3200 .F02a 4

Paper 5

Scripture 6

(I Do Not Write) About Nature 7

Water 8

Woman 9

Jupiter 10

Boom 11

Time 12

Margaritas 13

Dirt 14

She 15

Gaslight 16

Unit 17

Holy Inappropriate 18

Dwell 19

Allegory 20

Metaphorequiem 21

First Floor 22

Girlfriend in a Coma 23

Smile More 24

Bed 25

Unravel 26

Gallery 27

Anthology 28

Pine 29

Consumed 30

Yours 31

for Johnathan.
I love you, for always.

Opia

n. The ambiguous intensity of looking someone in the eye, which can feel simultaneously invasive and vulnerable...as if you were peering through a hole in the door of a house, able to tell that there's someone standing there, but unable to tell if you're looking in or looking out.[1]

[1] The Dictionary of Obscure Sorrows. (2013). Opia... [Tumblr post]. Retrieved from https://www.dictionaryofobscuresorrows. com/post/37651224370/opia

BLOW

I see the way you exhale,
your need
hitting the air like smoke—
a high
you remember softly at first
and then, with blunt force
against the walls of your reality,
a low
deep enough to ache
into past lives and constructed time,
feeling and fantasy
mixed in the same glass,
broken.
The swell in your chest
when she's near you—
between your fingers,
conversations resting
on your lips—
a slow burn so masterfully
short and intense.
Merciful.
You felt her once—
a dream or
a hallucination—
an evening descent
into the depths of your
mind, disappearing
as you breathe in.
You almost had her.

DESSERT

The words exited his mouth
slowly, like guests from a party
that had carried on
too late
into the evening—
Okay then.
The sounds of their footsteps
echoed in the corridor
of my ribcage,
the noise of small bombs
exploding with the force
of a thousand wars.
This war, too,
had been fought over land—
a plot the size of a fist,
borders the shape of a soul,
red as earth and
blood.

PS3200 .F02A

He sat in the stacks,
fourth floor, right.
The way his fingers touched pages—
without illusions,
without him paying for dinner first,
without him having to call
or at least say he would—
was better than the constant cold
spot on the other side of the bed,
the sight of the revolving doorframe
holding her silhouette,
the ring left on the nightstand
from a permanent whiskey glass.
The way his fingers
touched pages
was, for him, the love of a woman,
of a man,
of one that hadn't left him
smoking his last cigarette
at 2 a.m. on a Wednesday.

PAPER

This page stretches in front of me
as an empty bed,
cold sheets covered in hollow words,
no cover, no heat
from blankets or bodies.
Even hands on sheets
do not feel the same as hands
underneath them.
If you could turn this page,
would you?
Would you put new words along lines,
over them?
Would you like the way your name
feels on paper,
or when I read you aloud,
your syllables in echoes
on my tongue?

SCRIPTURE

You read me like scripture—
disbelief accumulating along the edges
of your mouth, alongside curiosity and
reverence
though none of these is strong enough
for you to close the book of verses
between us.
This church is an open grave
swallowing us both, consumed by dust
and naked,
reduced to the sacrilege of bones.
You said my name like scripture
and I saw you smile,
your teeth white as gravestones against soil.
Oh God.

(I DO NOT WRITE) ABOUT NATURE

because a flower is not a heart
and I feel no remorse for plucking one
or one hundred
from Earth's overgrown chest.
because your heart is not a flower
you did not give it to me
poised in a glass vase
as a symbol of
love or death,
fading, regardless,
from the center of the kitchen table.
because a flower is not a heart
I do not write
about nature.

WATER

I was only a reflection
in my own body
of water—
submerged to the waist,
split between quiet depths
and the refractory
glimmer of the fading afternoon.
I don't know how long you were there
watching and
I don't remember
the moment I stopped
sinking but
I remember the way I spread
out on a blanket to dry
in the sun like
laundry on the line,
new freckles dotting my skin
like flecks of salt on rocks
when the tide is out.
I don't know how long you were there
before
you were warm against
my chest, touching me
the way Spring does the flowers.

WOMAN

It caught me off guard
to hear you say it—*woman*—
like it was my name.

JUPITER

It's quiet here
in her orbit—
the vacuum of space
drawing him closer
and he'd never really wanted space.
No, he wanted her,
he wanted to taste
her shoulder, the red spot
he'd left this morning
revealing itself against the pale
of her skin.
He'd landed there without warning,
crashing through the atmosphere
and falling quickly—
slowly? surely—
into the hemisphere contained below.
Having the air squeezed out
of his lungs
the way she did it,
the way she ascended
left him breathless and
floating in her wake,
admiring the constellation of hips
and counting stars on the ceiling.

BOOM

Time sounds a lot like a bomb
when it's working
against you.
The words I've been holding
in are pressing on my hands,
making my fingers swollen
and clumsy as I try to decide
which wire to cut—
red, blue, yes, no?
I hear every damn second
ticking,
each one cold against my skin
as I try to make a choice.
My heart is still beating,
booming heavier and
slower than the seconds
but faster than I can speak.

TIME

I want to feel time
in small drops on my skin,
in streams when it runs down
my arm.
I want the only
hands on me
to be
yours
and the clock's—
I want the seconds to feel me
while I touch you.
I want the hours
to dig their nails into flesh
and hold on,
just a little longer.
I want to feel the weeks
in my knees,
my legs,
stopping me and running
over what's left.

MARGARITAS

Licking salt from the rims
of glasses, your lips—
your hands around thin stems
of glasses, my wrists—
the entire universe sits
in glasses.

DIRT

You've never looked better
than when you couldn't anymore—
when the soil hit the wooden lid
that finally stopped your gaze.
Does the dirt welcome you home
or did she reject you once, too?
Have I freed myself by forcing you
upon her, keeping freedom out of reach
for us both?
She will consume you the way you hoped
I would—taking you inside,
swallowing you slowly.
Let her take you, let her hold you
in your grave
until every one of your thoughts
has settled into the back of your skull
and dried like blood.

SHE

I needed her to feel me
the way she felt the words
on the page, on her fingertips
and lips ready to wage
war against injustices and
silence
against skin untouched—
I needed her to steady herself
against paper
and lovers worn, sturdy
beautiful and strong and
falling open in my hands,
letting me obsess over every line
every comma of her body, and her mind
reading her the way
I needed her to feel me.

GASLIGHT

She felt so far and still
he could see the fine hairs on her arm,
the purple freckles dotting her skin and wrapped
in sheets, her body the composer of
music he'd played so carefully—
silent, now.
She'd slipped away before,
an attempted intermission in the orchestra he composed;
she did not know—
she could not have known—
that he had done this all for her.
As she lay quiet and unmoving,
the glow of the light from the street below
cast shadows across his stage.
Tick. Tick. Tick.
Was this the metronome, keeping time
as he left notes scribbled across her neck
or the bomb waiting in his chest
to explode,
ripping him apart
and spreading him across her again,
showing her what was inside.
Isn't that what she wanted?
Isn't that what you want?

UNIT

With wires for veins
it's hard
to let the blood flow from heart to
head and back;
it's hard
to smile without
the filament bursting
inside a mouth.
With electric eyes
it's hard
to see the dark through
all the light;
it's hard
to rest when there is no switch.
With metal hands
it's hard
to feel warmth;
it's hard
to grasp skin under clothes.
With a switchboard torso
it's hard
to tell what's real;
it's hard
to know which line to
cut.

HOLY INAPPROPRIATE

You create gods from fingertips,
a sinner saved by
exorcisms strong and
devastating
like the release of demons.
Are you crucified?
Have you sacrificed your flesh
or only your thoughts?
You've painted patron saints
across cotton—
canvasses and mattresses—
they're all cathedrals
built from fire without brimstone.
You are no savior
but Lord do I
pray.

DWELL

What is my chest
but the hollow
into which you throw
yourself
after the spears of reality
have pierced your
raised hands?
You worship these gods,
idols
that line the walls of
your skull
like paintings in caves—
remnants of a civilization
contained against bone.
I've swallowed my words
a thousand times as
they linger against my throat,
pressed against my tongue—
a taste of intellect
and curiosity
defeated without the
satisfaction
of discovery.

ALLEGORY

Tolerability is dangerous
when it's you—
when it's a lie designed for peace
of mind, while wars are fought
against flesh, within these walls
my chest rises and falls
with your expression.
You know it, too.
Tolerability is dangerous
when it's messy,
when filler is no longer distilled
into something less.
Tolerability is dangerous
when it's more—
when time alone decided
your time alone.
You wouldn't be.
Tolerability is dangerous
when it's a match,
striking.

METAPHOREQUIEM

I miss seeing your thoughts
exploding across your face
like fire from a tossed grenade
fading now, distancing—
enemy lines retreating.
I heard a heart beating in your
desert
chest drumming like the footsteps of soldiers
marching to war and then
slowing,
stopping.
I watched your hands become machine guns,
as cool and strong as you ever were;
bullet fingertips pointed at strangers and you,
a mechanism, still feeling every shot.
I saw you crumble,
becoming sand—falling
in grains down to the bottom
of your own small hourglass.
I watched you run out
from underneath and mix salty with
tears, sinking into the red
sea, unparted.

FIRST FLOOR

I don't know how to write
this poem, I don't know
what it is
to feel so ripped apart—
my heart a piece
of blue construction
paper left in the hands
of a child learning his motor skills,
jagged edges trailing behind
untrained scissors and him,
smiling happily.
Were you happy, too,
when you smiled
holding scissors?

GIRLFRIEND IN A COMA

There's a coffee halo
drying on the paper,
and my heart is toast.
No more of your words
for breakfast;
I'll have to chew on my own
again.
Freshly squeezed
hands no longer start my day—
I'll be at the table,
watching the sunset first thing
in the mourning.

SMILE MORE

You can see my teeth
as I lay dying under dirt and flowers—
a garden blooming from my chest,
as my lungs no longer need the air to sigh
exhausted
in your direction.
Perhaps I will smile then,
unwavering as the flesh falls
from my face and my skull—
a body no longer assaulted
by any but the soil.
This ground is my mother,
her belly full of bones
of men who dropped dead like
flies on a windowsill;
I will rest here, as
you rot.

BED

I saw you there
with lips drawn like curtains
hanging behind
an unmade bed.
I'd slept there once,
waking next to that window
and wondering
where the night went.
I went with it,
chasing after the heat
of morning
and burning
my skin
on stale cigarettes
and the steam
from bad coffee
and wishing for one more night,
one more time
near that window
where the curtains hang,
drawn like lips
across teeth or panes,
behind an unmade bed.

UNRAVEL

I
want to
pull you like
a loose thread
from tapestry,
drawing each strand
slowly
out of your pattern,
watching you gather in long lines
around my fingers
as you
destroy yourself
against my hands,
unraveling.

GALLERY

What is art without the brush
of shoulders
in the hall,
strokes
on canvas
revealing themselves
like traitors to your imagination.
What is art without
the eyes of a patron
looking for significance,
finding beauty in a moment
in a frame
pressed carefully,
firmly, against the wall.
What is art
if you can't feel it,
if you can't touch it, if you can't
drag your fingers along the edges
of your favorite parts?
What is art but reverence
displayed with quiet abandonment
waiting for defiance.

ANTHOLOGY

How many times
have you tried to read this,
traced
your finger
along the title of
a spine,
lifting the cover to find
reality in the curves of
my breasts
and letters pressed against
skin and paper
bound in
your hands?
How long since you've read
your own work
or remembered what it's like,
since
your eyes
found meaning in lines,
since you poured a drink and sat quietly
with your thoughts or
maybe with mine—
how long has it been since you spread
a body
of work across your desk
and found yourself lost
between pages?

PINE

in my own dark woods
there are no bodies,
not like
you.
I talk with the ghosts
that echo soft reminders of
humanity through the pines—
I'm real,
for years or a day or maybe longer
it was real
it was all
real
wasn't it?
in my own dark woods
reality is only a word
but you,
you.
you are more than the whisper
hanging from a branch
and swinging lifeless in my memory
no you
are real—
I feel you
falling in pieces
like snow in the dark,
your presence
a fleeting line of footprints
disappearing into the landscape
in my own dark woods.

CONSUMED

I want to set you off
like dry brush suddenly aware
of the spark.
I want to watch you
acclimate to the threat
of my presence so close to you—
the fear in your throat rising with
the fire but, oh—
the way I'd writhe against you,
the way my flames would
lap slowly upward until they met
any part of you willing to give in
to the intensity
building between us—
I want to see your face
as you make sense of this dichotomy,
tinder against the heat.
I want to weaken you with every moment
I spend against you until
the moment you realize
how grateful you are
to burn.

YOURS

This one is yours—
this one
is the one you don't have
to question,
the one you can return to
on days you feel alone,
the one that will remind you
that you are someone
important.
This one is yours,
without you having to wonder
if your name is buried somewhere
in these letters—
this one
is *every* letter,
every smile that's formed
at the corner of your mouth and
lit up your eyes so quiet and subtle,
every hard-won laugh
breaking through the silence like a blade
of grass through a crack
in the sidewalk—
lovely, natural.
This one is yours.

With Thanks

There are several people without whom this chapbook would not be possible, and to whom I owe a great deal of thanks.

To my wonderful husband, Johnathan, who has patiently read hundreds of drafts of my work over the years and inspired so much of my writing. No one loves me better than you, and I love you more than anything. This one is yours, babe.

To my mom, Shelley, who has always encouraged and supported my creativity and who has believed in my writing since I was barely old enough to hold a pencil.

To my dad, Ken, who would have been so excited about this chapbook. Miss you, KT.
To my sister, Olivia, who consistently and wholeheartedly cheers me on and who always keeps me grounded.

To my amazing framily, who celebrate my victories as their own, who have loved me so well for the last decade and a half, who have workshopped with me, created with me, and grown with me all this time: Kailey, Amber, Skylar, Tabitha, Desirae, and Katie, thank you.

To my mentor, teacher, and friend, Marcus, who catalyzed poetry writing for me, who instilled a care for the craft in such a way that creating words became a biological necessity, a means of survival, a labor of love. Thank you, M.

To my family and friends who have each inspired, supported, taught, and encouraged me in their own ways: thank you for being part of this.

I'd also like to thank the editorial staff at Finishing Line Press for their support of Opia, and for their guidance in producing this chapbook. I am incredibly grateful for the opportunity to share this body of work.

Marjorie Sanders is an Alabama native who earned her MA in higher education administration from the University of Alabama, and her BA in English with a concentration in creative writing from the University of Southern Mississippi. Her poetry has appeared in publications from *Tempered Runes Press, The Bitchin' Kitsch, Assisi,* and *Product,* among others, and can also be found in anthologies including *Rebloom* (2020), *The B'K's Bitchin' Book* (2015), and *Tributaries* (2012). Writing is a uniquely human, uniquely social endeavor; after all, basic needs can be met without language, without formality. For Marjorie, poetry is a way to electrify the mundane; to make even the most basal experiences into something beautiful, or bloody, or breathlessly untamed.

Marjorie currently resides in Mobile, Alabama, with her husband, Johnathan, and their three dogs. In her free time, she enjoys traveling, reading about obscure historical events, and having coffee with Johnathan. That last one, especially.